The Spir

8 Games That W

There are some days in Celtic history that manage to stand above so many of the others and Saturday the 3rd of May 1986 was one of them. It may have poured from the heavens at Love Street but for the green and white clad supporters inside, it would have felt like the sunniest day of the summer.

Celtic were unstoppable that day but even a 5-0 lead wasn't enough to take the title until Albert Kidd fired home at Dens Park to put Dundee one up against Hearts. Kidd then grabbed a second to destroy Heart's title dreams and send Celtic into dreamland.

As the players and fans celebrated, a few interviews took place and Roy Aitken was in full-on cheerleader mode. When asked if he thought Celtic believed they would win the league, the bear replied

"We said with 8 games to go; if we win all 8 games, we'll win the league. We won all 8 games and we've won the league."

This is the story of those 8 games and how Celtic won the league in the final moments of the 1985/86 season.

Copyright 2011

Words: Andrew Reilly

Contents

Beware The Draws Of March 3

Demolition Job In Clydebank 5

Late Scare But Celts Hold On 8

Late Joy At Love Street 10

Celtic Back Into Fourth 14

Big Four Square Off 17

Aberdeen Stutter And Celts Can't Get Started 22

A Glimmer Of Light 24

And Then There Were Two 31

Celtic Versus The SFA 35

Job Done...Onto The Showdown 38

Championees...Championees 42

Consistency Against Bottom Teams Was Key 49

Beware The Draws Of March

The 4-4 draw with Rangers at Ibrox on the 22nd of March 1986 was immediately hailed as one of the best games between the two sides in a number of years and even to this day, fans of both sides have good memories of the game. Given that we were down to ten men for the larger part of the game and had fallen 4-3 behind, taking a point wasn't a bad outcome but it really should have been much more. Chucking away a 2-0 and 3-1 lead against Rangers is disappointing but in the greater scheme of the league season, it was perhaps a blow that could have killed us off.

Celtic were experiencing a terrible time in the opening months of 1986 and as thrilling as the 4-4 game had been, it did nothing to shake the fears that another season without the league was upon us. The end of the 1984/85 season had been brightened by the winning of the Scottish Cup in tremendous fashion but it was the league title that Celtic fans craved.

A failure to win the league since the 1981/82 campaign had been the longest the club had went without the league since the first half of the 1960s and it was becoming a source of much discontent amongst the fans.

There was to be no successful defence of the Scottish Cup, a 4-3 loss at Easter Road the week before the Ibrox match put paid to hopes of returning to Hampden and the league form was not inspiring either. After the Ibrox match on March 22nd, Celtic had played 10 league games in 1986, winning 3, drawing 6 and losing 1 with the league table showing us 7 points behind leaders Hearts, albeit with two games in hand. This would quickly move to being 9 points behind with 3 games in hand when Hearts defeated St Mirren 3-0 on Tuesday 25th March.

Celtic were inactive this midweek and wouldn't feature again until travelling to Kilbowie on Saturday 29th of March. This is how the top of the table looked going into this game.

Team	P	W	D	L	F	A	Pts
Hearts	31	16	9	5	51	29	43
D United	29	14	10	5	48	24	38
Aberdeen	29	13	10	6	50	25	36
Celtic	28	12	10	6	46	36	34

Demolition Job In Clydebank

After four successive league draws and a Scottish Cup exit, Celtic had to bounce back at bottom of the table fodder Clydebank. In the original fixture list, the game had been scheduled to be played at Celtic Park but the fixture in December had been switched due to the fact that Celtic had under soil heating.

Celtic won that game, as they had the two previous encounters with Clydebank that season, all without losing a goal. It was hoped that the same would happen at Kilbowie but at half-time, the score-line was 0-0 and those in the ground were not too impressed with what they were seeing.

The Celtic starting line-up that day was:

Bonner, McGrain, Whyte, Aitken, O'Leary, MacLeod, McClair, Paul McStay, Johnston, Burns and Archdeacon.

Even though the Bankies were lingering at the wrong end of the table, there was to be no relegation this season as the 10 team Premier Division moved to a 12 team top flight. This provided some degree of freedom for the Bankies and in the first half, they had the best chances. Bonner made up for a shaky performance the weekend before at Ibrox with a strong save from a Conroy drive. The Irish keeper then followed this up with a great stop from McCabe and it would be fair to say that the Bankies had the better of the first half.

If Celtic were looking to remain in the title hunt, they would have to improve and the difference in the second half at Kilbowie was as astounding as it was pleasing. A penalty in the 50th minute, converted by Brian McClair relieved a lot of the tension and pressure and the same player struck again four minutes later to double the lead. Derek Whyte had released the striker down the left hand side, with McClair finding plenty of time to drive home. Tommy Burns made it 3-0 on 58 minutes after some great work inside the box and McClair completed his hat-trick in the 67th minute, again scoring from the penalty spot.

Grabbing four goals in less than 20 minutes was an excellent return and although possibly harsh on the home side, it was exactly what Davie Hay was looking for from his side. Alan McInally completed the scoring with Celtic's 5th on 82 minutes and Celtic were back to winning ways. There would usually be joy at hearing news of a Rangers defeat but the 3-1 score at Tynecastle maintained the Gorgie club's 9 point advantage over Celtic, although Celtic held 3 games in hand over the league leaders. Then again, the mantra in football is that points on the board are the most important things..and the little matter of Dundee United and Aberdeen lying above Celtic in the league meant that many were not looking too far ahead in the title race.

March 29th: Top of the table results:

Clydebank 0 – Celtic 5   Dundee 0 – Dundee United 1

Motherwell 0 – Aberdeen 1   Hearts 3 – Rangers 1

Team	P	W	D	L	F	A	Pts
Hearts	32	18	9	5	54	30	45
D United	30	15	10	5	49	24	40
Aberdeen	30	14	10	6	51	25	38
Celtic	29	13	10	6	51	36	36

Late Scare But Celts Hold On

The win over Clydebank was to be expected but the manner of the second half performance was impressive. Celtic looked to continue this level of performance against Dundee at Celtic Park on a Wednesday night. In his programme notes for the game, boss Davie Hay summed the situation up:

"If we are to keep up our challenge for the Premier League title we must hope for others to slip up and at the same time make sure we don't slip ourselves."

Starting with the match against Dundee there were seven games left of the campaign and the chances of Celtic winning every game was unlikely...well, at least if you were basing your assumption on the results and performances of the 85/86 season so far. It was very much in hope as opposed to expectation that Celtic fans were travelling to games but 2 points in this game would draw Celtic level with Aberdeen and start to draw the hoops into contention.

The Celtic starting line-up that evening was:

Bonner, McGrain, Whyte, Aitken, O'Leary, MacLeod, McClair, Paul McStay, Johnston, Burns and Archdeacon

It was the same team which started at Kilbowie Park and a goal in the opening 20 minutes indicated that the team was carrying on where they left off. Maurice Johnston opened the scoring on 18 minutes and the lead was doubled just after half-time when Tommy Burns netted.

This was the score until 4 minutes from time when Ray Stephen grabbed one back for the away side, resulting in a nervy end to the match for the home crowd. There were thankfully no more goals though and the hoops were now level on points with third placed Aberdeen albeit remaining in fourth due to an inferior goal difference.

A crowd of around 12,000 was not totally unusual for this campaign and the fact that the match was played in midweek should also be taken into account. Davie Hay certainly wasn't ruling the team out of the title run-in but there was no over-riding sensation that things were happening just yet.

The stats for 1986 spoke for themselves and although the two wins on the bounce had been well received, it was going to take a good few more wins before people felt that there was a genuine title tilt in the current Celtic squad.

April 2nd: Top of the table result:

Celtic 2 v Dundee 1

Team	P	W	D	L	F	A	Pts
Hearts	32	18	9	5	54	30	45
D United	30	15	10	5	49	24	40
Aberdeen	30	14	10	6	51	25	38
Celtic	30	14	10	6	53	37	38

The league table after Wednesday 2nd of April

Late Joy At Love Street

It was Scottish Cup semi-final day and the four teams at the top of the SPL were in action. Hearts, Aberdeen and Dundee United fans were all excitedly looking forward to the games which gave their team hope of booking a place at the showcase final but Celtic fans were travelling to Love Street to see the hoops take on St Mirren in a league fixture.

In the Cup, Aberdeen trounced Hibs 3-0 at Dens Park whereas Hearts won a much tighter affair at Hampden, defeating Dundee United 1-0. John Colquhoun had grabbed the only goal of the game for the league leaders and there was genuine hope of a double for the maroons. Aberdeen fans were also in the same position with a league and cup double being a possibility but being seven points behind Hearts with two games in hand meant there were doubts about winning the league.

Of course, Celtic were also 7 points behind the league leaders at this stage with two games in hand but one of these games in hand would be played at Love Street. The Celtic starting line-up that day was:

Bonner, McGrain, Whyte, Aitken, O'Leary, MacLeod, McClair, Paul McStay, McInally, Burns and Archdeacon

It was Celtic that drew first blood when Murdo MacLeod launched a 20 yard free-kick into the net after 26 minutes and it was a lead that Celtic were fully deserving. It was a good start from the side but the loss of Alan McInally, not long before the opening goal came, through injury caused a large reshuffling of the team.

A look at the line-up showed that Mo Johnston was unavailable through suspension and Mark McGhee was out injured, leaving no fit strikers available on the bench. When McInally limped out of play, Peter Grant was brought on and Tommy Burns was shoved forward to support Brian McClair.

It had been a strange season for Tommy Burns who had spent a large part of the campaign playing at left back. This was not a popular move but no doubt boss Davie Hay felt that his hands were tied.

However, the introduction of Derek Whyte to first team duties allowed Burns to be placed back into the middle of the field and Celtic definitely benefitted from the experience and guile Burns brought to the side. Celtic may have lost their way a bit when Burns was placed up front but it certainly wasn't anything to do with Burns, who displayed a non-stop performance that was typical of his playing career.

Getting in at half-time a goal to the good was a relief for Celtic but it didn't take long for St Mirren to get back on level terms. Peter Mackie drew the Paisley side level on 56 minutes and it was probably a score that they deserved at that point. The Paisley side had their own injury concerns for this match but the returning Tony Fitzpatrick led by example and was responsible for dragging his team forward throughout the match.

With time running out, things were beginning to get desperate for Celtic. At this point, it was impossible to say if a draw would have been calamitous for Celtic's title hopes but it wouldn't have done the club any favours. In all honesty, the media were still fairly dismissive of Celtic's hopes of overhauling their three challengers at this point but on 87 minutes, Celtic found a way to grab both points.

A cross from the left hand side was flicked on by Brian McClair and Paul McStay was on hand to rifle the ball beyond Campbell Money and put Celtic back into the lead. The Maestro's late winner allowed Celtic to leapfrog Aberdeen and move level on points with Dundee United, although the Tannadice side's superior goal difference saw Celtic remain in second place. Both Dundee United and Aberdeen had a game in hand over Celtic but both of these teams would get to play this game in the midweek following the Scottish Cup semis.

With regards to the league, Monday's issue of the Evening Times stated that the bookies had cut Celtic's odds of winning the title to 8/1 from 12/1. Hardly a stick-on by any means but this was certainly a movement in the right direction.

April 5th: Top of the table result:

St Mirren 1 v Celtic 2

Team	P	W	D	L	F	A	Pts
Hearts	32	18	9	5	54	30	45
D United	30	15	10	5	49	24	40
Celtic	31	15	10	6	55	38	40
Aberdeen	30	14	10	6	51	25	38

The league table after the round of games on Saturday 5th of April.

With no midweek game to contend with, Davie Hay could turn his thoughts to the match against Aberdeen, on a day which many felt would decide the destination of the title.

"We started well on Saturday but then we tailed off. However we got the points and in our circumstances that was vital. So far as the game against Aberdeen is concerned, I don't think a

draw would suit either of us. We've got to keep this run going and hope that others slip up. So, it's interesting."

Interesting is an understatement but the midweek games would allow Celtic a clearer view of where they stood before the kick-off at Pittodrie.

Celtic Back Into Fourth

Both Aberdeen and Dundee United were involved in midweek after their Cup semis and both teams were going into the game on the back of differing results. Aberdeen sauntered past Hibs in their semi, booking yet another trip to Hampden for the 1986 Scottish Cup final.

Dundee United though had lost out at Hampden when a solitary John Colquhoun was enough to stop United's hopes of a Hampden final day victory. The memory of the painful 1985 Scottish Cup final defeat would no doubt have been fresh in the memory of United but they were to be denied the opportunity to finally clinch the old trophy.

If United were feeling sorry for themselves, they didn't show it as they destroyed St Mirren. Paul Sturrock opened the scoring inside 5 minutes with a stunning strike after he himself had cut in from the touch-line. United made it 2 just after the break when David Dodds tapped home after good work by Bannon and Sturrock.

It would be fair to say that Dodds was the unacceptable face of Scottish football with the playground style terracing chant mocking him mercilessly but he was a quality striker during his time at Tannadice. This goal came not long after Dodds and United announced that the striker was to leave the team in the summer and move to Neuchatel Xamax in Switzerland. The Swiss side had dumped United out of the Uefa Cup in this season but Dodds was unable to settle abroad for any length of time.

The youngster Kevin Gallacher grabbed United's third with Dodds scoring his second and United's fourth with Richard

Gough grabbing the final goal of the game late on. United may have been smarting at their Scottish Cup exit but were still perfectly placed for the title. United may have been 4 points behind Hearts but with a game in hand and the Jambos coming to Tannadice at the weekend, Jim McLean and the United fans leaving this game must have had genuine ambitions for another league triumph.

The Dundee United v St Mirren match took place on the Tuesday night with Aberdeen involved at Pittodrie on the Wednesday night. It was a lot tighter than the match at Tannadice but the home side managed to prevail in the end.

A 90th second opener by Jim Bett would had led many Aberdeen fans to think they were in the mood to rival Dundee United's demolition job of the night before and Frank McDougall made it 2-0 after 25 minutes with many thinking that the game was over. However, Motherwell shocked the home side by grabbing a goal back before half-time through John Reilly, who slipped the ball beyond Bryan Gunn in the Aberdeen goals. This lifted the Steelmen and Pittodrie was stunned when the away team grabbed an equaliser with less than fifteen minutes to go when Peter Kennedy bundled home the ball from a rebound.

Perhaps fearing what Alex Ferguson would have in store for them in the dressing room if they didn't win, Aberdeen found a second wind and managed to bundle home a winner through Peter Weir. It was a far more difficult night than it should have been for Aberdeen but the two points were vital and all eyes were focused on the biggest weekend of the Scottish league season.

April 8th and 9th: Top of the table results:

Dundee United 5 v St Mirren 0

Aberdeen 3 v Motherwell 2

Team	P	W	D	L	F	A	Pts
Hearts	32	18	9	5	54	30	45
D United	31	16	10	5	54	24	42
Aberdeen	31	15	10	6	54	27	40
Celtic	31	15	10	6	55	38	40

The league table after the midweek action of Tuesday 8th / Wednesday 9th of April.

5 points separated the top 4 teams and with all of the chasers having a game in hand on the leaders, there was no doubt that this was a run-in which was going to go right to the wire. The excitement and tension was at fever pitch and the fixture list managed to throw up an almighty day in the title race for Saturday 12th April.

League leaders Hearts would travel to Tannadice to take on second placed United whereas Aberdeen and Celtic were to square off at Pittodrie.

Big Four Square Off

In the space of just over a week, Aberdeen were to face their three rivals at the top of the league, with two of the three games at home. Given that the Dons had won the last two Premier Division titles and had just booked their place in the Cup final, confidence was high that they could pull out the stops when it mattered.

This was the backdrop of Celtic arriving at Pittodrie for a game that will live long in the memory of the hoops fans that travelled to Aberdeen.

The Celtic starting line-up that day was:

Bonner, McGrain, Whyte, Aitken, O'Leary, Grant, McClair, Paul McStay, Johnston, MacLeod and Burns

Yet another injury was to cause consternation in the Celtic backline with Pierce O'Leary succumbing in the first half. Owen Archdeacon was introduced to the play and this resulted in a big change to the Celtic line-up.

Derek Whyte moved into the centre half position, Danny McGrain swapped over to left back and Peter Grant dropped back to the right-back position. This meant that 3 out of the Celtic back four had switched from their original positions and Aberdeen nearly took advantage of these changes, narrowly heading over in the moments following the substitution.

This would have been massively unfair though as Celtic had started well at Pittodrie and had more chances than the hosts in the opening exchanges. Both sides, obviously knowing that a draw was no use to either's title challenge, were going for it and it was a surprise that there was no scoring before half-time.

It didn't take long for a goal to come in the second half though and it was Celtic who grabbed it.

Tommy Burns took a throw-in and Mo Johnston picked it up on the edge of the box and holding off two Dons defenders, fired a ball that flew into the bottom corner beyond Gunn. It was a tremendous goal and one that was rapturously received in the Beach End. This goal galvanised Celtic and the second half was played out predominantly in the Aberdeen half. Even with a hastily re- organised defence, Celtic looked calm and composed at the back with Derek Whyte giving a performance that was very mature for his age.

If anything, Celtic had every right to feel aggrieved at having a second goal chopped when Johnston again finished. A flag went up against Brian McClair who was in an offside position but was so far out of position that there was no way he could have been deemed to have been interfering with play, although this sort of call was pretty much left at the discretion of the linesman. Paul McStay also had a fantastic strike stopped by Gunn but Celtic held on for a fantastic win, which was the first time Davie Hay had seen his side triumph at Pittodrie.

Celtic had always been the outsider with regards to the title race but this result lifted Celtic clear from Aberdeen but any fan looking for news of a Hearts falter at Tannadice would have been in for a shock. Even allowing for the previous weekend's Cup defeat to Hearts, Dundee United must have fancied their chances in front of huge crowd in Dundee. A home win would have placed United on 44 points to Hearts 45...and crucially, the Tangerines would have had a game in hand.

Hearts were to give United a lesson with a victory that left most people convinced the title was Gorgie bound. John Robertson scored an audacious volley in the first half and as United pushed on to get back into the game, Hearts hit them with two killer counter-attacking goals in the second half. Sandy Clark and John Robertson grabbed the second half goals in front of a large travelling support from Edinburgh and to quote Chick Young; **"It edged Hearts to within inches of the title – and their fans knew it"**.

This should have been the warning sign for Hearts title push because Chick Young has never been a pundit with his finger on the pulse! Away from the top of the table, there was light relief for Scottish football fans when basement strugglers Clydebank triumphed 2-1 over Rangers at Kilbowie Park.

April 12th: Top of the table results:

Aberdeen 0 v Celtic 1

Dundee United 0 v Hearts 3

Team	P	W	D	L	F	A	Pts
Hearts	33	19	9	5	57	30	47
D United	32	16	10	6	54	27	42
Celtic	32	16	10	6	56	38	42
Aberdeen	32	15	10	7	54	28	40

The league table after the round of games on Saturday 12th of April.

The win at Pittodrie was a monumental victory, especially after the 4-1 capitulation at the venue earlier in the season. Celtic hadn't won at Pittodrie in the league since the 11th of December 1982, making for a few unpleasant trips home from the Granite City. The demolition earlier in this campaign had been particularly painful, taking place on a cold and depressing

November afternoon. An equaliser on the stroke of half-time by Davie Provan lifted the spirits briefly but Frank McDougall completed a master class of finishing in the second half to consign us to our second three goal defeat in a row.

This was the day when it was announced that Mark McGhee was arriving from Hamburg and much fun was aimed at the Dons fans with this signing but by the end of the 90 minutes, they were completely unperturbed about us buying McGhee. This game was of course the middle game of three 3 goal defeats we suffered as the promising early season disintegrated in a seemingly relentless run of defeats and draws.

That is why the trip to Pittodrie was definitely a "last chance saloon" game with respect to our title hopes and even though it was a hard-fought victory, it all turned out much easier than anyone could have predicted. It was an immense performance, especially when you consider the further injuries that befell the line-up and as surprising as it was in the context of the season, it was the exactly the sort of performance that Celtic teams have been known to muster when it was required.

Perhaps it is the passing of time but it seemed like the Celtic fans partied in the Beach End for a hell of a long time at the end of the game. The fans had no intention of going anywhere and the Celtic team had to come back out for an encore long after the Aberdeen fans had departed. Even then, the goal scorer was absent, later coming out by himself for a few moments. If you had told any Celtic fan at that moment that Mo Johnston would later go on to sign for Rangers and make himself the enemy it would have been the most ludicrous comment you would have heard in your life.

The thing is though; he is the one who has lost out not us. Thinking back on this game, his winner or the celebrations afterwards haven't been diluted by his actions, it was still an incredible performance and an almighty step on the way to the title. The only dampener on the day may have come when fans made it back to the supporters bus to find out that Hearts had trounced Dundee United 3-0 at Tannadice. A draw would have been the best result considering both teams were still in the running for the title but it certainly looked as though Hearts were going to take some stopping. Our 1-0 win at Pittodrie was an excellent achievement but you wouldn't have put any money on Celtic going to Tannadice and winning 3-0.

Although Hearts were dominant, watching the TV package later that evening one of the biggest highlights of the game came when Henry Smith made a stunning save from a long distance shot. The post-match analysis spent a bit of time going over the save and other vital stops made by the keeper and even though Hearts pummelled United in the end, Smith had a lot of good stops. It is fairly easy to look back on Smith and remember the countless blunders (and usually big blunders) in games against us but there was a spell when he delivered consistency in his goal-keeping.

The cry of "championees" was ringing out at Tannadice that day from the away end and most people were agreeing that the song was on the money!

Aberdeen Stutter And Celts Can't Get Started

Celtic were once again frustrated in their attempts to get their game in hand played away to Motherwell but the elements were not in the mood for assisting us. Yet again, there was a call off, this time due to a waterlogged pitch, so Celtic were once again left kicking their heels but United and Aberdeen squared off at Pittodrie.

The conditions at Pittodrie were not conducive to good football either and given that both sides had lost at the weekend, the mood at kick-off was not too bright. The mood got considerably worse for the home side before half-time when Gough volleyed United ahead. It was to be the only goal of the game as Aberdeen fell out of contention for the title, ensuring that the Dons would not achieve 3 in a row.

April 16th: Top of the table result:

Aberdeen 0 v Dundee United 1

Team	P	W	D	L	F	A	Pts
Hearts	33	19	9	5	57	30	47
D United	33	17	10	6	55	27	44
Celtic	32	16	10	6	56	38	42
Aberdeen	33	15	10	8	54	29	40

The league table after the midweek fixture of Wednesday 16th of April.

Two 1-0 home defeats had been a bitter blow to Alex Ferguson and the league was now officially beyond his team. With three games remaining, a 7 point gap was insurmountable regardless of what Aberdeen managed at Tynecastle but fans of Dundee United and Celtic were hoping that the Dons could bounce back and strike a blow to the maroon bandwagon that still no showed signs of stopping. This game was scheduled for the Sunday allowing United and Celtic to heap even more pressure on Alex McDonald and the Gorgie side.

With a World Cup looming and stirrings on the South side of Glasgow with regards a new manager; it wasn't surprising to find that a lot of talk in Scottish football was on matters other than the title race. However, a lot of focus was being placed on the Sunday match between Hearts and Aberdeen, with a larger than usual audience getting the opportunity to see the league leaders close up.

A Glimmer Of Light

The waterlogged pitch at Fir Park meant that Celtic were still a game behind their title rivals and fitting it into the schedule was not going to be easy. With a World Cup looming, there would be no extension to the league campaign and the Scottish national team had matches lined up for the last two midweeks of the season. Something would have to give and there were many hoping for Celtic's title challenge to fade away so the players could be removed without too much consternation from the club.

So, it wasn't as if there was enough pressure being placed on Celtic as they welcomed Hibs to Easter Road but the only pressure that mattered was the pressure to stay as close to Hearts as possible.

The Celtic starting line-up that day was:

Bonner, McGrain, Whyte, Aitken, McGugan, MacLeod, McClair, Paul McStay, Johnston, Burns and Archdeacon

The 2-0 score-line at Celtic Park suggested a comfortable victory but it was an incredible day of football with a large number of talking points. The first incident of the game came when Alan Rough moved far too slowly to pick the ball up from a pass back and Brian McClair jinked around him only to strike the post with the goal gaping. Seconds later Mo Johnston had the ball in the back of the net only for an offside flag to be raised against McClair, which stunned the crowd and the Celtic players.

Following on from a similar incident at Pittodrie, it was fair to say that Celtic's heckles were up. It was one-way traffic with Rough having to act sharply on a number of occasions to keep his side level. After the hour mark, Davie Hay introduced Mark

McGhee for Paul McStay as Celtic tried to go for broke and the Scottish internationalist quickly found himself with three chances to score, each one blocked by Rough. The much maligned goalkeeper was having one of those days when everything was falling in the right place for him and yet again Rough managed to break Celtic hearts by flicking the ball away from Johnston when the striker looked likely to score.

The substitution gave us more attacking power but it was the unleashing of Roy Aitken into midfield that finally spurred Celtic over the finishing line. Much like in the 1985 Scottish Cup final, when Celtic were in dire need of inspiration, Aitken was the man who would drive the team on from midfield building up wave after wave of attack.

It is easy to look back and think of the negative elements of Roy Aitken's game and how he was a poor centre half in comparison to the men at Tannadice and Pittodrie but how many times was Aitken the catalyst for memorable Celtic moments?

There are some fans who tell you that Aitken should be remembered as a hero for his performance in the 4-2 ten men won the league night alone. That was a thrilling performance with Aitken providing a dictionary definition of "taking the game by the scruff of the neck." The Scottish Cup final of the 1984/85 was also slipping away from Celtic until the Bear moved into midfield and breathed new life into the team...and eventually supplying the cross for Frank McGarvey's winner. It was to be this sort of performance that Aitken would deliver would against Hibs.

With little over 10 minutes to go, Celtic were pushing hard and it was the sort of tactic that left many fearing a counter-attack would completely undo the home side. Danny McGrain picked up a booking on 78 minutes and just as it was looking as though the win may be beyond Celtic, Mo Johnston created a chance for Owen Archdeacon who launched the ball behind Rough. Celtic Park erupted but then waited as the referee ran over to the linesman to discuss a possible offside decision.

It was an agonising wait but the goal was given and Celtic had the lead with 10 minutes to go.

With a few minutes left on the clock, Aitken scampered down the right hand side and fired the ball across goal where Brian McClair buried a header beyond Rough to make the game safe and keep up the faint hopes of a title win. This goal was Celtic's 7,000th league goal but its real importance here was in securing the win which kept Celtic on the tails at the teams at the top.

This win moved Celtic to within touching distance of Dundee United who managed to undo most of their good work at Pittodrie on Wednesday night. Disaster struck for Tangerines at Kilbowie where they were held to a 1-1 draw by Clydebank. For those who thought that United were the only team who could prevent the title from heading to Edinburgh, this result was all they needed to believe Hearts would take the title. A Hearts win at home to Aberdeen on the Sunday would see them move 4 points clear of United with four points left up for grabs for both of these sides. This match was also notable for being shown live on TV, the first Scottish league match to be shown live on television.

Many predicted that this would be the beginning of the end of football and although the official attendance of around 19,000 was healthy, it was 5,000 fewer than Hearts previous home game, against Rangers. Mind you, in the words of Wallace Mercer (upon announcing there was no need for segregation at a Tynecastle Scottish Cup tie for these two teams), these clubs "sang the same songs."

However, the travelling support from Aberdeen was probably weakened by their team being out of the title race and the live showing so there may not have been too many stay-away fans for the home club.

There wasn't to be a home win though, even if Hearts showed great strength and resilience to maintain their unbeaten record. Aberdeen were out of the title race but with a Cup final looming against Hearts, a positive result would have given them a boost for that game.

The Dons took the lead with less than twenty minutes to go with a Peter Weir penalty and it looked as though United would be given a reprieve for their slip in Clydebank...as well as giving Celtic added incentive to keep pressing on. However, with three minutes to go, John Colquhoun popped up to smash Hearts level and didn't the ground explode in celebration and relief.

This was Hearts trickiest remaining game of the campaign and taking a point, while not ideal, kept them firmly in the driving seat. Hearts knew that three points from their last two games would secure the title and even two points would see the title coming down to goal difference.

April 19th: Top of the table results:

Celtic 2 v Hibs 0

Clydebank 1 v Dundee United 1

April 20th: Top of the table result:

Hearts 1 v Aberdeen 1

Team	P	W	D	L	F	A	Pts
Hearts	34	19	10	5	58	31	48
D United	34	17	11	6	56	28	45
Celtic	33	17	10	6	58	38	44
Aberdeen	34	15	11	8	55	30	41

The league table after the round of games on Saturday 19th and Sunday 20th of April.

At this stage, the goal difference was:

Hearts + 27

Dundee United + 28

Celtic + 20

The fact that Dundee United held a better goal difference than Hearts would have been a concern for the Gorgie side but with two games remaining for these teams, United could only reach a maximum of 49 points. A win at home to Clydebank in their next league match would see Hearts move to 50 points making any goal difference advantage United held of no consequence.

Celtic had an extra game to claw back goals but with Celtic only being able to reach a maximum of 50 points and starting off 7 goals behind Hearts, it is fair to say that the Jambos were confident. If results went in their favour the following weekend, Hearts would be crowned champions at home.

Dundee were still to face Celtic and Hearts in the run-in and other results this weekend put Dundee into fifth spot, which would have been enough to earn a European place. The Dens

Park men destroyed Motherwell 4-0 at home at the same time as Rangers lost 2-1 at St Mirren. This ensured that the Dens Park men had 33 points from 34 games, one ahead of the team from Ibrox who had 32 points from 34 games. The remaining fixtures for these teams were:

Dundee: Away to Celtic, home to Hearts

Rangers: Away to Aberdeen, home to Motherwell

Rangers had a far superior goal difference to the Dens Park men so if the Dee were to grab a European spot, they would have to maintain their superior points tally. This gave Dundee everything to play for in their last two games.

The national team faced England at Wembley on Wednesday night with Roy Aitken in the side but a disappointing performance saw England triumph 2-1.

When examining the impact of the televised game on the Tynecastle attendance, it would be remiss not to look at the Celtic Park attendance for the Saturday match versus Hibs. It was a fairly low attendance for the Celtic versus Hibs match, listed as 15,996 and even though the Celtic end was closed off to allow work on the roof to be carried out, extending it to cover the whole terrace, it was obvious that not everyone believed Celtic would win the title. Crowds of this level were not out of the ordinary for matches like this, with a home game against Motherwell on the second weekend of the season having a crowd of barely more than 10,000.

This was in the era of children being lifted over the turnstiles and there were suspicions about the attendance figures that were released by Celtic but even allowing for all these shenanigans, many would draw an inference that many supporters didn't believe the team could turn the title race around.

There was nothing wrong with holding that opinion and who knows, it may have been shared by the dressing room itself but this was the 5th league game Celtic won in a row, having conceded only two goals during this period. That fact and the point that the team kept going even when it looked like it wasn't going to be their day to grab two goals in the final 10 minutes was a good enough reason to hang on in there.

And Then There Were Two

It was a nervy Tynecastle which welcomed Hearts and Clydebank onto the field but it was also an expectant audience, who knew that if luck was with them, the title could be celebrated long into the night. Hearts could only focus on their task and would have been mindful that it was the Bankies who knocked the United title challenge off the rails the week before but this was a much different proposition.

Gary McKay rifled the Jambos into the lead just after the half hour mark and it proved to be the only goal of the game. The last few moments of the match at Tynecastle would have been excruciating for the home crowd, who no doubt were tuned into the radio to hear updates from the other matches at the top of the league. There was to be no cause for celebration for the Gorgie home crowd.

Celtic were still managing to hang on in there and a 2-0 home win over Dundee meant that Hearts would not be crowned champions on this day.

The Celtic starting line-up that day was:

Bonner, McGrain, Whyte, Aitken, McGugan, MacLeod, McClair, Paul McStay, Johnston, Burns and Archdeacon

It was an unchanged Celtic line-up for this game and again, it was no straightforward win for Celtic up against a Dundee side hoping to pip Rangers for that final European spot. Finishing fifth would guarantee a place in Europe but Dundee knew they had matches against Celtic and Hearts, so they effectively held the destiny of the title in their own hands as well.

However, Celtic could only look after themselves, even if they would be reliant on someone doing them a favour. Davie Hay said in the build up to the Dundee game; **"We have three matches left and we simply have to win them all, even that may not be enough"**.

This summed the situation up rather well but knowing that they had to win all three games was firmly in the Celtic player's minds as they stepped onto Celtic Park that afternoon.

It was a nervy start for Celtic with Paul McGugan doing tremendously well to block Dundee after a quickly taken free kick but on the 20th minute mark, Celtic got a break. The visitors were reduced to 10 men after an act of absolute madness from Ray Stephen. The Dundee player was fouled by McGrain but a moment of lunacy saw him retaliate with an attempted punch at the full-back legend and there was only one option for the ref to take. Dundee were down to 10 men with 70 minutes of the game remaining and Celtic's hopes of eating into Hearts goal difference advantage looked to be alive.

Things don't always work like that in football though and it changed Dundee from being a team who were looking to attack when they could to one that was hoping to escape with a point. It was damage limitation for the team managed by Archie Knox in the hope that they could stay ahead of Rangers in the race for Europe. The Dens Park side managed to get to half-time with a 0-0 score- line and the fact that Hearts were winning at Tynecastle further dampened the mood at Celtic Park. If there was no change to the outcome of these two matches, Hearts would be champions at the end of the games.

As you would expect, Celtic found increased inspiration and fire to push on in the second half and in the 57th minute, the hoops made the breakthrough. Brian McClair worked a 1-2 with Peter Grant and elected to chip Bobby Geddes in the Dundee goal. With the aid of a slight deflection, the ball looped up and over the Dundee keeper to give Celtic the lead.

The crowd implored Celtic to push on and go for more goals but there was to be no further scoring until the 86th minute when Paul McStay and Owen Archdeacon engineered an opening for Maurice Johnston, who slammed home from inside the box.

At 2-0, the points were safe and one goal had been clawed back on Hearts. Celtic were still in with the slimmest of chances in the title race but that was not the case for Dundee United.

The Tangerine's bottle crashed at home as St Mirren grabbed a dramatic 2-1 win but even a win for the Arab's would not have been enough after Heart's win at home.

A home win would have seen United only capable of reaching 49 by the end of the season but the loss saw them stay on 45 points with just one game remaining. Second place was still achievable if Celtic slipped up in their two remaining games but to all intents and purposes, Dundee United's season ended here.

The hoops would travel to Fir Park during the week to finally play their rescheduled game and anything less than an away win would see Hearts crowned champions. A victory for the Glasgow side would see the title race go to the last day but even if that was to happen, Hearts were still viewed as clear favourites.

April 26th: Top of the table results:

Celtic 2 v Dundee 0

Dundee United 1 v St Mirren 2

Hearts 1 v Clydebank 0

Team	P	W	D	L	F	A	Pts
Hearts	35	20	10	5	59	31	50
Celtic	34	18	10	6	60	38	46
D United	35	17	11	7	57	30	45
Aberdeen	35	15	12	8	56	31	42

The league table after the round of games on Saturday 26th of April.

Celtic Versus The SFA

Continual call-offs had caused the Motherwell v Celtic game to be put back as far as it could go but the Scottish Football League insisted that the final day of the season remained the final day of the season. This left the last midweek as the only possible place to put the game and this meant that the Motherwell v Celtic match was to take place on the 29th of April.

The only problem was that Scotland were playing Holland in Eindhoven in a friendly that night, in their last match before heading off to the 1986 World Cup in Mexico. This led to a club versus country row and unsurprisingly, Celtic were the ones taking the flak for refusing to release three key players for an international friendly.

Alex Ferguson, national team coach following the passing of the late great Jock Stein, called up Paul McStay, Roy Aitken and Murdo MacLeod for the friendly match and insisted that they travel to Holland with the squad. This was to allow as much preparation time for the squad as possible and to assist Ferguson is announcing his final squad for Mexico.

The fact that Celtic were in the middle of a title race and had an all or nothing match at Fir Park on this evening appeared to matter little to the blazers at Hampden or the media. In an article in the Evening Times dated 28th April 1986, Alan Davidson and Graham Clark managed to come up with this paragraph which outlined their thoughts on the matter:

"It is almost beyond belief that Alex Ferguson has been left without the Parkhead trio because Celtic have to play Motherwell at Fir Park in a rearranged League match crucial to the Glasgow club's title hopes."

Surely the paragraph should have read that it is almost beyond belief that Celtic would have been robbed of three vital players for a league match crucial to their title hopes so Scotland could play a friendly match?

SFA President David Will continued the hyperbole by stating;

"To lose them in such circumstances just a fortnight before we set off for the World Cup is almost unbelievable. I will want to know just what has happened when I return to Scotland."

To place this into some form of context, the Holland v Scotland friendly was to take place on April 29th. The last round of league fixtures was to take place on May 3rd. The Scottish Cup final, featuring Aberdeen managed by Alex Ferguson, was taking place at Hampden on Saturday May 10th.

Scotland would not play in the World Cup until the 4th of June, over a month after the last league fixture. Given the closeness of the title race, it is obvious that Celtic would be unwilling to release these players and any other club in the same position would have did the exact same.

Boss Davie Hay made the following quotes about the situation;

"I don't care what anyone says, Celtic are blameless. In fact, we have bent over backwards to help Scotland, Motherwell and everyone else."

"We were prepared to leave the game until next week when there would have been no problem but the League ordered the match to go ahead."

"We have always said that if we were involved in the Championship then we would obviously want these three players."

"I phoned Alex Ferguson on Friday and again – in the company of League President Ian Gellatly – on Saturday night. There was no suggestion that the players staying with the club would be a problem."

It would have been interesting to see if Alex Ferguson would have been so keen to spend time in Holland for an international friendly if Aberdeen were involved in a final day shoot-out for the league title. As it was, the Dons hit a slump in April, freeing Ferguson from any such concern but the fact that Celtic were intent on taking the league to the wire was obviously a problem for many in the game.

With the three players in the squad and no doubt ill wishes from football fans all across the country, Celtic headed to Fir Park desperate for a convincing win which would force a final day resolution to the title.

Job Done...Onto The Showdown

Again, this was a night when Hearts could have cracked upon the champagne to celebrate a title win but the onus was all on Celtic to grab the two points and score the goals that would give them a glimmer of hope on the final day. Anything but a win would have made it impossible for Celtic to overtake Hearts and of course, Celtic were also 6 goals behind Hearts when it came to goal difference.

This match was originally meant to have taken place on the 1st of March but a number of call-offs saw it eventually played out in the final midweek of the season. When the game was originally meant to be played, no one could have predicted how crucial this match would become in the final shake-up of the Scottish season.

The Celtic starting line-up that evening was:

Bonner, McGrain, Whyte, Aitken, McGugan, MacLeod, McClair, Paul McStay, Johnston, Burns and Archdeacon

This was the third game in a row this line-up started and it was hoped that a settled line-up would be a key factor in the final few games of the season. Celtic set out to attack but as is often the case with Celtic, particularly in the 1980s, this left glaring gaps at the back for the opposition to expose on the counter-attack. Motherwell had a few chances in the game, even at 0-0 and if it was not for Bonner, the final score could have had a very different complexion.

It is easy to see why some fans idolised the big keeper whereas others thought he was nowhere near good enough for the Celtic goalkeeping jersey. He was a very likeable man and had a great ability to stop shots that seemed destined for the back of the net. Conversely though, he had a major weakness on cross balls and his kicking was suspect at best. It was probably best for Bonner that his career was winding down when the back pass rule came into play but on this night, like at other times during the run-in of the 85/86 season, Paddy was at his best.

One of the problems for him was that he was no Jim Leighton but equally, Bonner did not benefit from having a McLeish / Miller or Narey / Hegarty partnership playing in front of him. Over the course of this game, Paddy stopped from Reilly on a couple of occasions and also held well from Baptie.

Another factor that usually caused Celtic fans to moan about the outcome of the match was the referee and it took until the third strong Celtic penalty claim for the bhoys to be awarded with a penalty.

At 0-0, Murdo McLeod was flattened inside the box but referee McCluskey was having none of it and waved away the appeals. Some justice was done minutes later when McClair poked home the opener but given that Celtic could only win the title on goal difference, every decision was being examined closely.

Another big decision came in the second half when Maurice Johnston went down in the box but this time the man in black ruled that it was the Celtic forward that committed the foul and gave the free-kick to the home team. The exasperation of the Celtic fans and team was starting to show but then a double whammy of an incident which saw Owen Archdeacon go down in the box and what appeared to be a handball from the Motherwell defender left McCluskey with no choice but to award Celtic a penalty.

Brian McClair stepped up and rattled it home to effectively seal all two points from the match but there was a desire to push on for more goals. Celtic continued to press forward and should have made it three- nil late on when substitute Mark McGhee had a shot blocked by the keeper and McClair, in the hunt for a hat-trick, could only force the rebound against the bar.

For the third game in a row, Celtic ground out a 2-0 victory and this win at Fir Park meant the title race would go to the last day. Both teams challenging for the title would be away from home, Hearts travelling to Dens Park to take on Dundee and Celtic returning to Love Street to take on St Mirren.

April 30th: Top of the table results:

Motherwell 0 v Celtic 2

Team	P	W	D	L	F	A	Pts
Hearts	35	20	10	5	59	31	50
Celtic	35	19	10	6	62	38	48
D United	35	17	11	7	57	30	45
Aberdeen	35	15	12	8	56	31	42

The league table after the midweek fixture of Wednesday 30th of April.

At this stage, the goal difference was:

Hearts + 28

Celtic + 24

All Hearts had to do was avoid defeat and the title would be bound for Gorgie. For a team who had gone 27 league games undefeated, this didn't seem like the hardest task in the world.

However, even if there was a major shock at Dens and Dundee managed to take the two points, Celtic had to win and also have a four goal swing in their favour. If Dundee won by 1 goal, Celtic had to win by at least 3 strikes. If Dundee won by 2, Celtic had to win by 2. If Dundee won by 3 or more goals, any victory for Celtic would do. Hearts were huge favourites on the morning of Saturday 3rd of May 1986.

Championees...Championees

The rain was pouring down in Paisley and it just seemed to emphasise how mad we all were, turning up in the slight hope of a party but likely facing disappointment. The official attendance was listed as 17,557 but with the customary lift-overs and a door being forced open at the away end of the stadium, it was fair to say that Love Street had attracted a reasonable crowd for the final league game of the season.

It wasn't the only big crowd that day though as Dens Park posted an official attendance of 19,567 with a large number of those fans bedecked in maroon and white. Nothing was impossible in football but surely nothing could stop Hearts now...not when they were teetering on the brink of success.

Hearts fans had a boost with the news that top Dens striker Ray Stephen would miss the match due to suspension, ironically for the red card he received at Celtic Park. Hearts were also able to recall their own captain, Walter Kidd, who had sat out the previous game due to suspension.

The Hearts line-up that day was:

Smith, Kidd, Whittaker, S Jardine, Berry, McDonald, Colquhoun, I Jardine, Clark, MacKay and Robertson

It was near enough as strong a Hearts line-up as you could have picked at the time although Craig Levein was an absentee. After the game, Hearts boss Alex MacDonald said that Levein had been laid low by a virus, which also affected a number of players in his starting line-up. Maybe it was a virus, maybe it was nerves but regardless of this, Hearts knew what they had to do to take the title.

Hearts also knew that the bookmakers were listing Celtic as 6 to 1 outsiders for the title.

Davie Hay was well aware of what his side had to do;

"Scoring the necessary amount of goals is not beyond us. We know of course that St Mirren are not going to sit back and let us score but if we display the same attitude and form of recent weeks, it should be good enough."

What Hay said was perfectly correct and the reference to it being 'good enough' was only with reference to what Celtic could do. A three goal margin of victory was not beyond Celtic and if they achieved it, they could at least say they did everything within their power during this run-in to take the title.

The Celtic starting line-up that day was:

Bonner, McGrain, Whyte, Aitken, McGugan, MacLeod, McClair, Paul McStay, Johnston, Burns and Archdeacon

An early goal from a corner got Celtic off to a flying start, Brian McClair excellently nodding home an Owen Archdeacon corner, swung in from the right hand side. McClair found space expertly in the box, losing his marker and timing his run perfectly to nod his header past the helpless Jim Stewart, who was in goals for the Buddies that day.

This start was exactly what Celtic needed and the fans, already roaring their backing for the bhoys, managed to lift the volume further. The shed enclosure was packed, with many fans seeking refuge from the rain but it became a surrogate Jungle for the day, providing the starting point for many of the songs and chants. In saying that, behind the goal, exposed to the elements was pretty vocal as well.

Looking back now, everyone is quick to point out how rubbish St Mirren must have been but this was certainly not the case. Even before McClair netted, the Buddies were involved in and around the Celtic box and at 1-0, it was an open game. To merely state that St Mirren were poor would also be doing Celtic an almighty disservice as it would not be overkill to say that Celtic were phenomenal in the first half at Love Street.

In saying that, this was not matched by the score line after half an hour but two strikes in the space of a minute soon rectified that small problem.

Brian McClair won a scrappy bouncing ball in the middle of the park and slipped it to Paul McStay, who intelligently fed Mo Johnston, who appeared to have the freedom of the right hand side of Love Street. The striker powered his way into the box unchallenged and fired a shot that squirmed in underneath Stewart to make it 2-0. This was exactly what was required and the fans were still singing when the game had restarted and the ball found its way into the Celtic box.

There then followed what remains the greatest Celtic goal this writer has ever been fortunate enough to witness.

Danny McGrain, on his own 18 yard line hooks the ball inside to Murdo MacLeod, who returns it to McGrain who had made his way out of the box. Danny tucked it up the line to a deep lying Paul McStay, who controlled it, beat his man and fed Aitken.

The Bear, in one touch, fed the ball onto Danny McGrain who had continued his run, overlapping both McStay and Aitken. McGrain, now just inside the St Mirren half, played the ball further up the right hand touchline to Brian McClair, who nonchalantly nutmegs the St Mirren defender and runs by him to the edge of the Buddies box.

With his next touch, Choccy sidefoots the ball into the box in the direction of the on-rushing Maurice Johnston, who calmly finished from the 6 yard line.

On any given day, it would have been a goal of such majesty and confidence that it would be talked about for years to come but to create a goal of this standard in a match of such magnitude was almost beyond words. Celtic knew they had to win by three clear goals but no one said they needed to score one of the greatest goals that football had ever seen to do so.

At this point, you were convinced that the league was coming back to Paradise, goals of that standard can do that for you…but of course, the reality of the situation soon returned.

If it dawned on the fans though, it didn't appear to have dawned on the players as Celtic grabbed a 4th before half-time. All of the goals had been created down the right hand side until this point but for this strike, Owen Archdeacon made his way down the left- hand side and cut the ball back where Murdo MacLeod was seemingly well placed. He must have had a shout from behind because Murdo overstepped the ball, letting it run through his legs where Paul McStay came in and fired the ball into the back of the net.

4-0 to Celtic at half-time in what had been an absolutely breathless 45 minutes of football. It appeared that the same could not be said for Dens Park, where nerves seemed to be affecting both sides, although Hearts could point to a couple of misses from their normally reliable front pairing.

If the score line from Love Street filtered its way through to the Hearts dressing room, it would have been understandable if some nerves crept into the Hearts line-up but the title was very much still in the Jambo's hands.

It was unlikely that Celtic could be as majestic in the second half and like the first half; the initial chances fell to St Mirren. Paddy Bonner made two good saves at 4-0, the second one seeing him picking up an injury for his hard-work but it actually served as a jolt to the Celtic team.

The 5th goal was a bit lucky, Murdo MacLeod having a tame shot from outside the box expertly steered home by McClair, for his second of the game, and a 5-0 cushion was more than enough for Celtic. No doubt realising that there was no more that they could do, the Celtic players settled into a more containing role. There were not many chances for either side as the game petered out with the hoops fans straining for news from Dens.

There was a notable moment around the hour mark at Dens Park when Vince Mennie struck a stinging shot through a ruck of players but once again, Henry Smith was up to the task. Even knowing the score in Paisley, this save seemed to galvanise the Hearts support, who raised the volume in an attempt to drag their boys over the line.

With Rangers winning at Ibrox over Motherwell, there wasn't much incentive at Dens for the home side to force the win and this looked like being enough to deny Celtic the title. However, on this craziest of crazy days, rumours sprang around Dens that Tommy McLean's Motherwell side had equalised at Ibrox and that a European spot was up for grabs. Sensing their time had come; Dundee found a second wind to attack Hearts and with 7 minutes to go, forced a corner on the right hand side.

The ball was swung in high and deep with a Dundee head knocking it down to the six yard line, where Albert Kidd absolutely buried it. The home fans erupted at Dens as the Hearts fans behind the goal slumped in disbelief.

At the same time, a cross ball into the St Mirren box was easily taken by Stewart, which led to one of the most remarkable scenes in Scottish football. As perfectly captured by the Scotsport cameras and beamed around the country the following day, Stewart had collected the ball and was calmly standing when the terraces around him erupted.

The outpouring of joy at the goal was massive, after all, it was what everyone had been waiting, hoping and praying for. The action at Dens had become far more important than what was happening on the field in Paisley but there was still time for Hearts to grab an equaliser and take the title which many believed was theirs.

At least, this is what a lot of Celtic fans would have reasoned but Hearts were shot, a team that had been hanging on in there desperate to get to the full-time whistle had their hopes and dreams ripped away from them with no response available. In fact, when the Hearts players were looking for the ref to show mercy and put them out of (or perhaps, into their) misery, Kidd worked a one-two and fired home his second goal to ensure the league trophy would have green and white ribbons on it. As the volume of cheers at Love Street increased, there was confusion over whether the final whistle had gone at 1-0 or if it had been a second goal for Dundee.

In the grand scheme of things, it didn't really matter and when ref Andrew Waddell grabbed the ball on the half-way line and signalled the end of the contest at Love Street, Celtic fans flooded onto the pitch.

It was a remarkable win, a win against all the odds and a victory deserved both on the day and in the run-in. Yes, there would be a lot of sympathy directed towards Hearts but it's hard, even to this day, to take anything away from a Celtic side that strung together 8 wins in a row and also managed 16 league games without defeat.

In fact, Celtic's last league defeat came on the 4th of January in a 4-2 defeat at Tannadice. There were far too many draws in the months of January, February and March but just when it mattered the most, this Celtic team found its form and strength...and the title.

May 3rd: Top of the table results:

Dundee 2 v Hearts 0

St Mirren 0 v Celtic 5

At the end of the season, the top of the table looked like this:

Team	P	W	D	L	F	A	Pts	GD
Celtic	36	20	10	6	67	38	50	29
Hearts	36	20	10	6	59	33	50	26
D United	36	18	11	7	59	31	47	29
Aberdeen	36	16	12	8	62	31	44	31

Consistency Against Bottom Teams Was Key

Although the 8 game winning streak at the end of the campaign is eventually what won the title for Celtic, it was the consistency against the teams in the bottom half of the table that helped us finish up at the top of the pile.

The results against the other challengers were very poor, failing to defeat Hearts or Dundee United at all in the season. In saying that, three draws against Hearts were probably pivotal in the final reckoning, none more so than the last minute equaliser by Paul McStay at Tynecastle on the opening day of the season. Similarly, a Mark McGhee equaliser in Gorgie on the 14th of December also turned out to be crucial in taking the title on the final day. It also started McGhee's habit of scoring vital goals versus Hearts while wearing the hoops.

Results for the 1985/86 season:

Celtic v Hearts

1-1 (A), 0-1 (H), 1-1 (A), 1-1 (H)

Celtic v Dundee United

0-3 (H), 0-1 (A), 2-4 (A), 1-1 (H)

Celtic v Aberdeen

2-1, (H), 1-4 (A), 1-1 (H), 1-0 (A)

Celtic v Rangers

1-1 (H), 0-3 (A), 2-0 (H), 4-4 (A)

This meant that against the rest of the top 5, Celtic played 16 league games, where they recorded 3 wins, 7 draws and 6 defeats. This equates to winning 19% of these games, drawing 44% and losing 37% of these games. Celtic picked up 13 points out a possible 38 against the remaining 4 teams from the top half of the league.

This is certainly not title winning form but the biggest factor in taking the title was consistency against the bottom 5 teams in the League:

Celtic v Dundee

2-0 (A), 3-1 (A), 2-1 (H), 2-0 (H)

Celtic v St Mirren

2-0 (H), 1-1 (H), 2-1 (A), 5-0 (A)

Celtic v Hibs

5-0 (A), 1-1 (H), 2-2 (A), 2-0 (H)

Celtic v Motherwell

2-1 (H), 2-1 (A), 3-2 (H), 2-0 (A)

Celtic v Clydebank

2-0 (A), 2-0 (H), 2-0 (H), 5-0 (A)

This meant that against the bottom 5 teams, Celtic played 20 league games, where they recorded 17 wins, 3 draws and 0 defeats. This equates to winning 85% of these games and drawing 15% of the matches. Celtic picked up 37 points out of 40 points available from the 5 teams in the bottom half of the league.

Another big factor in being able to overturn Hearts came in the horrendous opening quarter of the season the Edinburgh side had.

In their opening 9 games of the season, Hearts only recorded 2 wins although this would have been 3 if it were not for that Paul McStay equaliser at Tynecastle back in August. No one knew then just how important that goal would be but if Hearts fans felt aggrieved at not taking the points from this game, their next league match left them shell-shocked.

A 6-2 defeat at Love Street suggested it would be a long season for the Jambos with a 3-1 defeat at Ibrox in the next league making matters worse. A 2-1 win in the Edinburgh derby followed this Glasgow defeat only for hopes of a revival to be cut short by Aberdeen who knocked Hearts out of the League Cup and then defeated them 3-0 at Pittodrie in the league.

Respite came with a 2-0 win over Dundee United but Hearts completed the first quarter of games by losing 2-1 at Fir Park, losing 1-0 at Kilbowie and drawing 1-1 at home to Dundee. This draw would set Hearts off on an unbeaten run which would span 31 games. The run started against Dundee and it ended against Dundee on the final day of the season. Considering that Hearts had only picked up 6 points from 18 in the first quarter of the league, no one could have expected them to go on such a lengthy unbeaten run and they definitely deserved credit for their efforts in this season.

The run-in to the season was also played out against the backdrop of Graeme Souness and Walter Smith being installed at Ibrox and this was occupying the media as much as the destination of the title. Rangers were in absolute dire straits at this time, capable of raising their game against Celtic but so often failing against lesser lights.

After the 4-4 draw at Ibrox on March 22nd, Rangers had 5 games to play, winning only once. This final day triumph against Motherwell allowed the club to sneak into Europe just ahead of Dundee but defeats to Hearts, Clydebank and St Mirren, as well as drawing with Aberdeen, indicated how desperate the Ibrox side were for change at the top.

What was to follow at Ibrox, and the failure of Celtic to spend to match the new era is a completely different story but the 80s up to this point had been an abject failure for Rangers.

The media is quick to praise the success of the 'New Firm' in this decade and while it would be churlish to downplay what Aberdeen and Dundee United achieved, it is felt as though this media outlook was carried out to minimise the poor showing of Rangers. The 85/86 triumph was Celtic's third title of the decade (following triumphs in 80/81 and 81/82) matching the three of Aberdeen (79/80, 83/84 and 84/85), although the Dons did have three Scottish Cup triumphs and the European Cup Winners Cup to show for it. With Dundee United picking up the league flag in

82/83 and also showing well in Europe, a neutral observer would be inclined to state that three Scottish teams were strong in this period.

Celtic will probably look back at some capitulations and the inability to build from the back as a reason for not having won more league titles or for failing to progress further in Europe but the Celtic side of this era was still one that was capable of great moments. However, the triumph in 85/86 can viewed in isolation as one of the great periods when the club pulled together and managed to confound its critics.

Even now, 25 years on...and after suffering a few final day heartaches in the intervening years, the spirit shown by the 85/86 Celtic side was a perfect embodiment of what many believe to be the Glasgow Celtic way.

Attacking play underpinned by a combative spirit fuelled by being the underdog and looking to prove people wrong is a feature written through the club's history and will no doubt be as much of Celtic's future as it is their past. Individual members of the 85/86 team may have tarnished their memories in certain ways (and not just the obvious one) but regardless of what has happened since, the memories of this title triumph remains the stuff of legend for Celtic fans everywhere.

Printed in Great Britain
by Amazon